A **MIND** IS A TERRIBLE THING TO
MANIPULATE

NARCISSISTIC ABUSE:
The Psychological and Emotional Torture You Don't See Coming

MICHAEL SUNSET

ISBN: 978-1-09831-302-9 (print)
ISBN: 978-1-09831-303-6 (ebook)

INTRODUCTION

If you're reading this book, you likely already know what the Cluster B personality disorders are. The Cluster B is made up of narcissistic personality disorder, antisocial personality disorder, which consists of sociopathy and psychopathy, borderline personality disorder, and histrionic personality disorder. In this book I'm going to tell a personal story of what it was like getting psychologically, emotionally, and financially abused by my ex-spouse. As part of this abuse I also endured a brutal smear campaign that was led by my sister, my mother, and my ex-wife along with her parents. I will also go into detail on how a person or group of people with Cluster B personalities can put you in the hospital or lead you to feel suicidal without laying a finger on you. I'm hoping my experience of going through severe emotional manipulation and abuse, mainly in the form of gaslighting, will be able to help others to defend against it. I will explain what gaslighting is along with what a smear campaign is. I will also give real life examples of how to identify these abuse tactics and how they take place. I've learned there are many people out there that have had similar experiences with their own family, friends, a significant other, at the workplace, or in a family they married into. I feel my experience was an extreme situation, but I'll let you be the judge of that.

The experience of getting mobbed, scapegoated, bullied, gaslit, and smeared by numerous people that I loved and thought loved me had harmful effects on my psychological, emotional, and physical health. I endured an excruciating amount of psychological and emotional pain from the gaslighting and smear campaigns once my marriage was falling apart that literally almost killed me. This included a misdiagnosis of bipolar disorder from a mental health practice that was manipulated by my wife, my mother, and my sister. I didn't realize how long a smear campaign could last for and how to defend against one. I wasn't even aware I was a part of it and didn't know when or where it began. It was understandable that my ex-wife would be running a smear campaign against me when our marriage was failing, but my own mother and sister running smear campaigns of their own didn't make sense. What would they have to gain by doing that? I'll explain how I learned that it's just part of who they are and part of their personality to engage in this behavior.

I was forced to put a strong emphasis on self-care and form-
ing healthy coping strategies. I strongly believe having healthy
boundaries in relationships is key for anyone's overall health. I will
discuss hitting rock bottom of toxic relationships and how I was
able to build myself up to the point where I was strong enough to
fight for more parenting time with my daughter and prepare to
defend against more gaslighting efforts and smear tactics.

My rocks that kept me going and saved my life are my identical twin brother and my beautiful daughter. I want to dedicate
this book to them along with other narcissistic abuse survivors
around the world. My daughter gave me the strength to take
care of myself so I could take care of her and give her the best
parts of me to the best of my ability whenever she is with me to
this day. My brother helped to ground me in reality without him
I'm not sure how long I would have been questioning my sanity
for. Therapy was also a key component to recovering from my
experience with toxic relationships. I've learned that all of these
personality disorders are most likely responses to environmental
trauma with a genetic predisposition. The worst part about them
is that they usually cause a lot of pain and trauma in the people
closest to them. My experience will hopefully give you a reason
to get out of the abusive relationship if you are in one and never
go back as I will explain it could be fatal if you don't.

This book is based on my opinions, perspective, and recollection of events that took place in my life. I realize that the people

I describe in this book may have a different opinion and recollection of the events I describe. In no way is this book meant to harm anyone. It is meant to inform victims, targets, and survivors of how harmful narcissistic abuse can be. I'm hoping that it will help other victims of narcissistic abuse to be able to recognize it, become more aware of it, and be better equipped to deal with it.

CONTENTS

Chapter 1: Narcissistic Abuse and Smear Campaigns 1

Chapter 2: Valentine's Day: Love and Money 6

Chapter 3: Gaslighting and Projection 19

Chapter 4: The Covert Narcissist Sibling 25

Chapter 5: Bipolar or Psychological and Emotional Abuse? 35

Chapter 6: Finally Divorced 54

Chapter 7: Not My Reality 58

Chapter 8: High Conflict Lawyer 62

Chapter 9: The Importance of the Share Nothing Plan 66

Chapter 10: Family Therapy 75

Chapter 11: Malignant Narcissism and Psychopathy 78

Chapter 12: Psychological Testing and Custody Evaluation 83

Chapter 13: Healing and Recovering 94

CHAPTER 1

Narcissistic Abuse and Smear Campaigns

For anyone that has been in a relationship with a narcissist or other Cluster B personality disordered individual, you were in a one-sided relationship. Overtime you most likely learned that you barely existed in that relationship. Narcissistic abuse refers to any abuse by a narcissist, particularly emotional abuse in relationships. The impact of narcissistic abuse on its targets or victims can be difficult for mental health professionals to distinguish from mental disorders. Many victims will show signs and symptoms of Post-Traumatic Stress Disorder, Complex Post-Traumatic Stress Disorder, Acute Stress Disorder, Depression, Anxiety Disorders, an Adjustment Disorder, or a Situational Depression. This is one of the reasons a narcissist is successful at making you out to be the crazy one to family and friends. Your emotions will be all over the place justifiably so. They will do this by starting a smear campaign or distortion campaign against you, which is an all-out attack on your character as well as your mental health. They will use any information they can against you and are very good at doing this. In my case my wife, both her parents, my sister, and my mother were successful in getting me to doubt my perceptions of reality. They convinced me and others that I was selfish, paranoid, manic, irrational, and had some form of Bipolar Disorder. It was a very confusing time where I suffered a great deal of anxiety and depression symptoms from this sick form of psychological and emotional abuse. There is no way I could have seen the psychological and emotional torture coming because I was born into it and conditioned to it. Many people don't see it coming because they want to see the good in others; it's very hard to see one of these predators coming. They are very good at luring people in and hooking them into relationships using their superficial charm.

Smear campaigns have been identified as a common weapon of sociopaths, psychopaths, narcissists, borderlines, and histrionics. A smear campaign is an intentional, premeditated effort to undermine an individual's or group's reputation, credibility, and character. A smear campaign is a character assassination. Smear campaigns usually target government officials, politicians, political candidates, and other public figures. I'm living proof that a smear campaign could happen to anyone. A great movie to watch that breaks down exactly how a smear campaign works and that it could happen to anyone is *Enemy of the State*. This movie with Will Smith as the target shows the best thing to do during a smear campaign is to stay out of sight and out of mind. Anything you say and do can and will be used against you during a smear campaign.

The best thing you can do is to not defend yourself to anyone; it's best not to give rumors any attention. Of course, this is a lot easier to see after your life has been flipped upside down and you're trying to make sense of what is happening. After you survive one, you'll be better prepared if you ever have to face one again. I made many mistakes during the smear campaign but eventually would take the proper steps to shutting it down and getting my life back. It's important not to talk to people that are friends or family attempting to explain your side of things that often speak to the narcissistic individual or people engaging in the smear. A narcissistic individual will attempt to get to anyone close to you and flip the smallest things around to get people to question you and doubt you. If an abuser can't control the way you see yourself, they will try to control the way others view you. In my case they were getting me to question my sanity along with the people I was closest to, including many mental health professionals.

So, what do you do when you find yourself in the middle of a smear campaign? The natural reaction is to fight and defend yourself. Mine began on 22 March 2016 that I know of but most likely began before that. I have finally come up with something I call the "Share Nothing Plan." Verizon has the "Share Everything Plan", that's what I used to do because I had poor boundaries, but the only way to defend against a smear campaign is to share nothing. Its important to share nothing personal and show no emotion when interacting with anyone engaging in the smear campaign. I worked myself into exhaustion attempting to defend against my smear campaign. This landed me in an Intensive Outpatient Program fighting for my life to dig out of a severe depression. My smear campaign was started by my ex-wife and my sister working in tandem. I'll get into the details of how they did that and how hard they worked to successfully pull this off. The lies and rumors spread fast and quickly around town, to friends I grew up with, family, my college friends, and anyone else that knew me well. My mother and sister somehow got just about everyone. The lies and manipulations were very convincing; even I believed some of what they were saying. I believed them because I put my full trust in my mother and sister. This was a decision that would almost kill me. I believed I was the problem, and I had this severe mental illness, and if I listened to them my problems would get better. They were my family; I had no reason to believe they would steer me in the wrong direction. They say mom knows best but for anyone that has a narcissistic mother, unfortunately, you know that's not the case.

CHAPTER 2

Valentine's Day: Love and Money

It was Valentine's Day of 2016 and my wife at the time had been on short term disability with a flare up of her gastrointestinal tract where she was out of work for about six months and immobile for much of this time. She spent many months sleeping on our couch in the living room. It killed me to see her like that, and when I would try to talk to her, she wouldn't open up to me to talk about it. I asked her if I could bring her to her doctor's appointments when I was available, but she wouldn't let me go to any of her doctor's appointments. She would always go with her mom. I would make breakfast most mornings, offer her breakfast in bed, but often she was too sick to eat. I was ready to do whatever it took to get through this rough time for both of us. Looking back, I don't think she wanted me to see her in the condition she was in because she wasn't perfect and didn't think I would accept her. I loved her, no matter. She had to take steroids and other medications that were tough for her body to handle. I didn't have a problem with that. I wanted to be close to her, but she put up a wall and wouldn't let me get close to her. When I reflect back, I see she was always emotionally unavailable just like my mother. That's why I went for her; I just didn't realize it the whole time we were together. I felt needed by taking care of her every want and need, which is not healthy. It is a sign of codependency. My issue of being codependent developed in childhood where all of us were taking care of my narcissistic mother's wants and needs. Attempting to make a narcissist happy is a full-time job where it is not possible to be successful. It didn't matter what my father, twin brother, older brother, or sister did. We all were destined to fail at this job. My relationship with my wife would eventually get to that same point. Our relationship was at a place where I was looking to learn and grow in the relationship. Narcissists aren't capable of looking at themselves and asking what can I do to improve myself or a situation. As I learned more about narcissists, I found there is no amount of love, affection, money, validation, or attention that will ever make a narcissist feel whole and satisfied. They always need more to attempt to fill their empty void. They don't see an issue with their behavior so if you have an issue with it you are the problem, they aren't going to change for you or anyone else. My wife and I were growing more and more apart as time went on because of this.

We went out to dinner on Valentine's Day; she was feeling much better and about to go on vacation with her mom to Florida. She was also being encouraged by her doctor to go back to work. While out to dinner on Valentine's Day my wife dropped a bomb on me. She said, "Do you think you could take $50,000 out of your trust fund so I could stay home and focus on my health?" I had a trust fund with about $90,000 in it at the time. I had already put about $43,000 into real estate, this included a starter home that wasn't good enough for her and her parents. I had also withdrawn money to pay for my master's degree from this fund. My stress level immediately went through the roof. I was already feeling a tremendous amount of stress living a lifestyle I didn't care for. Why did I feel this was such an unreasonable request? She knew I was stressed about money when we moved into a bigger house, but she wanted what she wanted. She didn't care that I wasn't comfortable. I felt if I gave her the $50,000, there would soon be nothing left of the trust fund. I told my twin brother I felt like a minnow in a shark tank that could be swallowed up whole along with my bank account at any time. This isn't how a person should feel in a marriage. We had a beautiful two-year-old daughter at home and most of the caretaking duties and disciplining were on me. Having a child together I was committed to doing whatever we had to do to work things out. I had the trust fund thinking we would use it for emergencies and I did not feel this was one of those times. I was thinking more on the lines that we could use the money to send our daughter to college one day. To be able to afford the lifestyle we were living and the bigger house we both had to work. I let her know this when we purchased the house and she agreed to that. It was one of those times where she was telling me what I wanted to hear so she could get what she wanted – A common narcissist tactic. When we bought the house, she also agreed to cut back on her spending, but instead of cutting back, it was greatly increased.

It had been a stressful year and a half for us and I wanted to take her out for dinner at a nice restaurant in hopes things would start to get back to when we were first married. Going out for overpriced dinners was always of high priority to her. I wanted her to be happy so if we could afford it, I was willing to do it even though I didn't care for going out to the nicest restaurants. Rather than get back on track, our relationship would take a turn from that day forward that I never could have imagined. I was unaware she associated love with money, but it was becoming pretty clear that was the case. I personally don't see any correlation between the two. Having the best of everything was important to her and I always tried to sacrifice to meet her wants. She always had to have expensive things such as designer clothes and shoes with the best brand names. She also enjoyed going on the best vacations. In her mind she was entitled to all of these things. Everything had to be the best, and for a while, I was the best in her eyes and the eyes of her parents. Soon I was going to go from the best to the worst. Also known as the idealize, devalue abuse cycle. I felt relieved she was being encouraged to go back to work by her doctors. There was no way I could cover our lifestyle and the high mortgage on my teaching salary. I also felt relieved her physical health was returning and I would have the wife I fell in love with back, or so I thought. I wanted her to open up to me and talk to me about how she was feeling along with the financial request of $50,000, but she would say things such as, "Money is your problem were not allowed to talk about it." This is a classic example of stonewalling, which is a relationship killer for anyone in any relationship. Stonewalling is a clear refusal to communicate. I remember saying to her, "I feel like there is a terrorist attack on our bank account every week." I calculated she spent around $2500 a month after all bills were paid. If I brought it to her attention that I didn't agree with certain purchases, she would throw in my face that she made more money and I would eventually back off to keep the peace. I was a people pleaser, which I would later learn is also toxic. I had to learn about my codependency issues and take ownership of how my issues contributed to the unhealthy relationship dynamic. Being an enabler or a codependent is toxic. I can now clearly see that my father is a codependent and an enabler in regards to his marriage with my narcissistic mother. The dysfunctional relationship dynamic is all I knew from being a part of it growing up. Although I wasn't aware of this until recently. I had learned many unhealthy behaviors as a result of this. If I was healthy, my relationship with my wife would have ended much sooner. Getting out of an unhealthy relationship with a narcissist and getting to a better place is a slow and painful process. Once you do that, you'll most likely be very cautious and avoid getting into another relationship with a narcissistic individual.

I felt a great deal of pressure building with financial stress since I was strongly encouraged to buy a $323,000 house in August of 2014. This was a huge jump after being in a starter home that cost $192,000 with very manageable payments. I had been anxious and uncomfortable from the day we moved into the bigger house in September 2014. The weekend we moved I had a take home midterm exam for the first course of my master's program that I didn't have much time to work on. I was frustrated we were moving everything into a house I could care less about to try to please my wife. I heard numerous times from numerous people, "Happy wife, happy life." My wife would never be happy or satisfied is what I didn't realize at the time. I thought I was the man for the job to make her happy and be responsible for her happiness. I've learned no person is responsible for another person's happiness. With a narcissist their happiness depends on the time of day and if they are getting what they want. If you do something to upset them you might be punished and not even know what you have done to upset them to deserve the punishment.

My anxiety was up from the day we moved into the house, and it would slowly increase as time went on. Prior to purchasing the bigger house my wife asked me if I could use the trust fund money for the down payment on the bigger house. I let her know I wasn't comfortable because I wanted to use a portion of that money for my master's degree while we had low house payments on our starter home. Before I met her I didn't use that money for much of anything; I didn't even think about touching it. I think back to only being married a few months and she was hounding me to get her name on the trust fund. I actually inquired about it but the people I had the money invested with talked me into not doing that, thankfully. My wife went to her parents and they offered us a gift of $56,000 dollars for the down payment on the bigger house. I wasn't allowed to talk about this to anyone. I told her it didn't matter whose money it was I wasn't comfortable purchasing the house. She said, "You're not going to tell me how to spend my parent's money." I lost the argument, threw my hands up and said, "Ok we'll see how it goes." This purchase would increase our expenses by about $1,000 a month even though we were getting a nice gift; I didn't want the gift of unnecessary financial stress.

Looking back, I realized the night I said no to the $50,000 was one of the only times I said no to my wife. I bent over backwards to do what she wanted to do and to make her happy for our roughly three-and-a-half-year marriage up to that point. But that night on Valentine's Day I said how I really felt that I wasn't comfortable buying the house in the first place. I said, "I'll sell this house before I give you $50,000." My wife said she would never sell the new house. I believe that was the right move to draw the line somewhere and set a firm boundary for the first time with her. I had no idea how badly I had been taken advantage of financially up to that point. I had a lot of anger, resentment, stress, anxiety, and frustration built up about buying the house along with how I was being treated in the marriage. I had gone to bed angry many nights. I know that I allowed many of the things I was upset about to happen. I signed for the bigger house and was always accommodating. The way decisions were made was that it was her way or the highway. A narcissist, sociopath, or psychopath will slowly push your boundaries and take advantage of you over time and make you think it's your idea. They will say and do many things to you that you didn't invite them to do, nor would you believe a human being is capable of doing to another person. There is a saying don't go to bed angry, and it had happened too many times, something had to change. I wasn't happy for about the year and half we lived in the new house except for the time I got to spend with our daughter; she brought a lot of joy to my life.

The symptoms I was starting to display were all stress related but many people I loved and trusted would spin my stress related symptoms and distort my reality. Starting in March 2016, a lot of work was being done behind my back by my sister and my wife that I wasn't aware of. I was in for a smear campaign or distortion campaign from hell that would impact my life in a way I never would have thought possible and I had no idea it was coming. It would also impact the time I got to spend with my daughter. Was I the problem? Was I an ungrateful person for the wonderful gift of a down payment on a dream house from the in-laws? Was I a selfish, insensitive husband? I could see how things would look this way to people on the outside that didn't know the whole story. My wife was sick for months with a gastrointestinal disease, it's not about me. I should be there to support her and give her any amount of money to get through the difficult time, right? I felt if I gave her the money, there would be nothing left in any of my bank accounts soon after. I believe my gut feeling was right about that. I had already sacrificed way too much of myself and my money up to that point. I gave so much because that's who I am, but the love, care, and respect was never reciprocated because my wife wasn't capable of that. This is what takes place when you're in a relationship with a narcissist. They are able to mirror you and reciprocate initially, but eventually withdraw becoming cold and distant, displaying their true selves over time. It appears that a narcissist is not capable of true intimacy in relationships. Your left wondering what happened to the person you fell in love with. This was the norm for me to unconditionally love people that weren't capable of loving me back because I grew up with two emotionally unavailable parents. You learn to accept putting in a lot of effort and not receiving much in return.

When we bought the new house, I took $5,000 out of the trust fund for granite counter tops and to paint just about every room in the house. I had already put $38,000 down on the starter home including the closing costs. Prior to selling the old house I repainted every room in that home with the same color paint that was already on the walls as requested by my wife. We re-glazed the bath tub, refinished the hardwood floors, put a new oil tank in, new hot water heater, new counter tops, new tile backsplash in the kitchen, and much more. We did all this to turn around and sell the house for a loss after living there for just a few years. We agreed to live there for at least five years, but after just three years she was ready for bigger and better. Everything has to be new and improved; with a narcissist there is always a new house project they are pushing for.

My wife felt entitled to her parents' money, my paychecks, my savings accounts, my trust fund, my parents' money, nothing was off the table she wanted it all and felt it was hers for the taking. Narcissists are entitled; they live a parasitic lifestyle. My wife loved spending other people's money even though she made good money. I felt I was being stretched as far as I could and I had to make a stand. I had no idea what I was in for by simply standing up for myself. My wife's parents got wind of arguments taking place between me and their daughter. They wanted to speak to me and I wanted to speak to them. In the middle of March 2016, I had gone to see a Psychologist for therapy because according to my wife I was the problem and needed help. The Therapist described me as logical, reasonable, level headed, and committed to solving issues in my marriage. He told me I needed to bring my wife in with me. As I mentioned money was my problem and we weren't allowed to talk about it. I also felt I was being disrespected in many ways not just financially. For much of our relationship if we argued about something and it made me feel awful, she would tell me not to talk to anyone about it. I know now this is something abusers do. They want you to keep quiet about the abuse. If you don't, they will do everything in their power to attempt to silence you. In the relationship, I would usually apologize for some abusive thing she did that made me feel awful, so we could move on from it. I had no answer for all the money my wife was spending and how I could make up the difference if she didn't work. She was doing less and less overall while I took on more and more. This didn't happen overnight, it slowly took place over time. There were many red flags in the beginning but I kept telling myself she'll be reason-able, and she tells me how much she loves me so we'll always be able to work things out.

The Psychologist had a very logical solution for our money issues. He said, "Anytime two people make different amounts of money you take a percentage of each persons' income, for exam-ple 60 percent of each person's income and put that into a joint account to pay bills. The other 40 percent you keep in your own accounts and do what you want with it." He said that was really the only way to do it. I was looking to save some money because we weren't saving anything. We were actually dipping into money I had already had before entering the marriage. There was no reason for this, we brought in around $7,500 a month. My wife's parents have a lot of money and she wanted to live their lifestyle. Her parents would take us out to dinner, cover hotel rooms, go on extravagant vacations along with many other things. I remember a time her mother went up to the front desk at a Marriot hotel and said, "I'm a gold member and this room is not up to my standards." This is how she talked to people on a regular basis. I didn't pick up on it in the beginning but it started to make me sick how they treated staff at restaurants, hotels, and people in general. Narcissists believe they deserve special treatment not just from their significant other but from everyone. We are all here to serve them. I strongly believe this is how they think. The main issue for me was their cups were never going to be full; it didn't matter how many things or vacations they had, they always wanted more. They were draining me psychologically, emotionally, and financially. It was exhausting to try to keep up with them and be around them. I could feel I wasn't good enough for them and their daughter even before we got married. There was nothing I could do to ever be good enough is how I felt.

Going back to me being the problem, I've learned narcissists are never wrong, and if something goes wrong someone has to be blamed for that, and that lucky person was me. This is called scapegoating. Growing up in my house my dad was always the scapegoat for all of my mother's issues. My older brother was the main scapegoat out of me and my siblings, but anyone could become the scapegoat and get ganged up on at any time. This is what happens in a narcissistic family. I never knew that we were a narcissistic family but, it's very clear now. I also never could have imagined that I would marry into an even more of a narcissistic family than my own family. I never thought I could be the scapegoat and get mobbed by members of both families at the same time when I needed support the most. Prior to my marriage falling apart I was very independent and never asked for help or support from anyone for the most part. I was at a point where I needed a great deal of help solving the issues in my marriage. The next step was to go to marriage counseling with my wife. I also felt trying to reason with my wife's parents was important since they were such a big part of our lives.

CHAPTER 3

Gaslighting and Projection

The term gaslighting comes from the play *Gaslight*. In the play a narcissistic husband who is also psychopathic slowly manipulates his wife into believing she is going insane. The reason he manipulates his wife into believing she is losing her sense of reality is so he can commit her to a mental institution and steal her inheritance. This is exactly what my wife attempted to do to me with the help of her parents, my mother, and my sister. I'll explain the events leading up to this along with the continued gaslighting efforts by all of them to not only attempt to gain control over my finances, but to also gain control over our beautiful daughter.

On 25 March 2016, which was Good Friday, I arranged to go over to speak to her parents about the overwhelming circumstances and things I was stressed out about. Her dad owns his own business in Sales and has a lot of money. He is very arrogant, grandiose, impulsive, reckless, a pathological liar, lacks empathy, lacks guilt, lacks remorse, is deceptive, ruthless, manipulative, has a weak conscience, and is never wrong. He could sell anything to anyone by exploiting their weaknesses and vulnerabilities. Dr. Ramani Darvursala a leading expert on narcissism mentions in a series on Medcircle that psychopaths make the best salesman. He was one of the best salesmen for sure. My wife had a very similar personality to him and has a high-level job in the corporate world in Finance. This is where you will find many narcissists and psychopaths at the top of corporations. I always thought that being a psychopath meant you were a serial killer that was most likely in prison. Psychologist Robert Hare, who developed the psychopath checklist, is also the author of *Without Conscience: The Disturbing World of Psychopaths Among Us and Snakes in Suits* teaches us that many people that are high in psychopath traits are living among us and are very successful financially. They are obsessed with money, power, and control. My ex-wife's father is very condescending and lets you know in more ways than one that you're beneath him. When I walked into their house, he was in the hallway pacing and appeared to be angry, his face was red. I sat on the couch and he began unloading on me saying, "I'm disappointed in the way you're treating my daughter." He also said, "Now I know why your brother said he felt you were becoming a better person in his best man speech, you're not a very good person." He told me I had an anger problem and I was a liar despite the fact that I never lied to them or my wife about anything, not one thing. I continued to get screamed at and berated being told I was "irrational" multiple times. This was projection and exactly who he was, although I didn't know it at the time. I believed him that this is who I was because of my tendency to be self-doubting.

I told him that I felt overwhelmed and it was taking everything out of me to live a lifestyle I could care less about. I also mentioned his daughter spent around $2500 a month after all of our bills were paid and she talked to me about getting a job to provide for a family. I mentioned that all of our money was going in one direction and that was out the door.

I asked her dad, "How does spending $2500 a month after all our bills are paid help provide for a family?"

He walked away into the kitchen and said, "I'll have to talk to her about that."

I mentioned, "I had a two-bedroom house that I could afford on my own. Why would I move? The increase in stress and expenses doesn't make sense to me. I can't handle paying for the house on my own with her spending habits and I'm not comfortable giving her $50,000."

Her father sat back and said, "Let me tell you something about money; you can always generate more money."

Her mother chimed in with, "That yard was too small for Marie and you know it."

I said, "Too small for a one year old," even though our daughter was actually 10 months old at that time.

Her father then proceeded to tell me, "That house was a loser, a two-bedroom house is a loser."

When we lived there, I always felt it wasn't good enough for them. The house was great for a lot of people but not for them and their daughter. According to my wife and her parents, we weren't like everyone else. We were above the general population. That's the narcissist mindset. Back when we were discussing purchasing the bigger house and he could see I wasn't comfortable with the idea of purchasing it, he said, "Let me tell you something about houses in Connecticut, your house can get foreclosed on and you can just walk away, the bank can't touch you." This did not make me feel any more comfortable about purchasing the house, but it was a good sales line.

The conversation continued. I said, "Let me tell you what the therapist said that I went to see."

Her father cut me off and said, "That guy doesn't know you."

I attempted to speak again and he cut me off screaming, "Bullshit, bullshit, bullshit, who cares, who cares, who cares." So I couldn't utter a word. To him, this conversation was about dominating me into submission, and he eventually accomplished that. I can see this now when I reflect back on the conversation. Then the gaslighting came in strong even though I had never heard the term gaslighting.

He said, "These mental illnesses manifest themselves differently. You need to be evaluated by a team of Psychiatrists. You've always had these psychological and emotional problems. You at least have anxiety. Members of your family said that you could be Bipolar."

I immediately knew this was my sister and I said, "Who said that? My sister? She's been waiting to take a shot at me for years." This is what my gut feeling was and I should have trusted that.

The verbal beating continued a little more. He gave me a hard time for every decision I made, such as buying a used truck. The verbal beating finally ended when I broke down crying because I couldn't figure out why they were talking to me like this. I had gone over there to have an adult conversation and attempt to work things out.

Then he threw in a mind fucking statement at the end, "But we like you."

I said, "Thanks for the support guys, this year has been a walk in the park." I had to pull myself together and go pick my daughter up from daycare.

Looking back, I can see now this was all gaslighting and projection from her father. It was difficult to make sense of what they were saying because I looked at them as a second set of parents. They psychologically, emotionally, and verbally beat me.

They basically told me I was worthless, no good, and mentally ill. This hurt like hell. This is what narcissists do to control others – Make them doubt themselves and question their sanity. This confirmed the beliefs that were instilled in me from childhood by my narcissistic mother. According to all of them, I was irrational and mentally ill, which is textbook gaslighting that a narcissist or other Cluster B would use. I trusted them so much that I believed most of what they said. I knew my marriage was most likely over after this but I still had the mentality I'll do whatever I have to do to make the marriage work. They wanted it to work but for them working meant manipulating, controlling and abusing me. I was just unaware of this at the time. The therapist I was seeing was trying to tell me I was being abused. I didn't know this at the time either. I was in denial of that and thought these people loved me and I loved them. I was siding with the abusers for a while, and I would continue to do that for way too long. At least I had a loving, caring, and trusting mother and sister is what I thought. I'll get into the gaslighting from my own mother and sister along with the toll it took on me psychologically, emotionally, and physically.

CHAPTER 4

The Covert Narcissist Sibling

My wife told me she would go see the therapist I found, but she wanted to speak to him first. On 22 March 2016, just three days before the verbal beating from my wife's parents, she went to see the therapist. He called me before the appointment and said, "Michael, is it ok for your sister to be here?" I was shocked and really caught off guard that my sister was there. This was a blindsiding I didn't see coming, but there would be many more to come from my sister from that day on. I should have said no to keep my sister away from manipulating any mental health professional. This would have saved me a lot of pain and suffering. It may have been a blessing in disguise that in the next few years my sister would reveal who she truly was, a person I couldn't trust that was fully invested in tearing me down very covertly. I've heard the covert narcissist is also called the fragile or vulnerable narcissist. I feel covert is fitting because these types of narcissists have a covert aggressive personality. Meaning they are very sneaky in their acts of anger and aggression. Most of their attempts to hurt others are done behind closed doors or behind people's backs, so there isn't a lot of proof of their abuse. My sister's involvement in my situation was a crucial part of me hitting rock bottom of toxic relationships and finally saying enough is enough of this sick form of abuse. I said yes to her being there at the therapist's office with my wife that day. I told him, "I have nothing to hide," even though it didn't feel right. I was told they discussed issues about our finances and they found he was not a competent therapist. The reason for this is because they couldn't manipulate him. According to them our finances were fine. I was still the problem and needed a psycho-logical evaluation. I still trusted my sister so I agreed to this. I would later learn a year and a half later when I would go back to this therapist that the two of them attempted to convince him that I was having a manic episode of Bipolar Disorder. He would later tell me, "They did not have your best interest in mind." He also compared my sister's behavior to treason. My sister had this theory that he doesn't know me and wouldn't be able to see the psychotic, manic episode I was having. In reality he wouldn't be able to notice I was having a manic episode of Bipolar because I wasn't having one. I had increasing levels of stress and anxiety at the time that's for sure. Going in for a psychological evaluation increased my anxiety even more. This is exactly what gaslighting does to a person. It induces anxiety. You will have emotional flashbacks, heightened anxiety, intrusive thoughts, a low sense of self-worth, mental confusion, and in severe cases it can lead to suicidal ideation or a suicide attempt.

My twin brother and I would eventually nick name my sister Judas. This was fitting since she played a large role giving my wife and her parents false information that they basically used to crucify me, which started on Good Friday of 2016. When we were kids my sister would always tell on me and my brothers if we did something wrong, as a result we nick named her "Rat Bastard." This was probably when we were around 12 years old and she was around 10. I never thought she would live up to the nick name and then some in adulthood.

It was the day after Good Friday and the verbal beating from my wife's parents, I went out to the Salmon River to do some trout fishing and clear my head. This was a place I would go often to be at peace to relieve stress by getting out in nature. I was not at peace on this day; I had severe anxiety and what my wife's parents said to me was playing over and over in my head. I was also obsessing over why my sister was making me out to be mentally ill and what her and my wife were discussing with the therapist. I was going to pick up a steamed cheeseburger on my way home for dinner. I called my wife to see if she wanted one and she said her parents were coming over for dinner. I told her I didn't want to see them.

They were always involved in just about everything we did and were quite overbearing. I felt like I was married to three people. They controlled just about everything in my wife's life and now controlling many things in mine as a result. For example, where we lived and what we ate for dinner many nights. I felt like I was a servant that worked for my ex-wife and her parents. I was even dressed up and told what to wear much of the time. I needed a break from them especially after the verbal, psychological, and emotional beating, which was worse than most physical beatings looking back. I would rather get physically beaten and put in the hospital for a couple months then go through what I was about to go through. Neither form of abuse is ok, but this type of abuse was hard to detect for anyone experiencing it, which is why it is often called hidden abuse. It has longer lasting negative effects compared to a one-time physical beating. It's possible for people to experience both forms of abuse from an abuser over a prolonged period of time which will give just about anyone Complex Post-Traumatic Stress Disorder symptoms. I was in my truck ready to take off and go home during the phone call. Her parents were the last people I wanted to see so I put my fishing gear back on, got back in the water and fished until dark. Anytime I could get away and do some fishing I would usually stay out on nice nights until dark because it was so peaceful. I dreaded going home where I would have to walk on eggshells and hear the negativity about being out doing something I enjoyed. This would happen on a regular basis no matter how long I was fishing for. I always took a lot of crap for it when I got home. If I went out to play pickup basketball games, the same thing would happen. I had talked to a friend about how this would happen and he said, "Tell her I'll be home when I get there." I thought this was a funny comment but I was never like that. I always let her know what I was doing and gave her a time of when I would be home. On my way home I got my steamed cheeseburger and waited until I knew her parents would be gone before I went home.

Starting the next day, I would randomly break down crying uncontrollably and fight to pull myself together. The constant negative messages were really sinking into my mind and poisoning it. Breaking down and being emotionally messed up was my mind and body processing the abuse. The next day was March 27, Easter Sunday. We were supposed to go to the country club my wife's father belonged to for Easter dinner. That morning I was breaking down and crying right in front of our daughter. I was a mess. I was trying to pull myself together and process all of the things that were being said to me. My wife screamed at me saying, "You're crying in front of your daughter. What the hell are you doing?" She said her and my sister had been trying to figure out what's wrong with me. This was an example of a complete lack of empathy along with continued gaslighting efforts. This was just the beginning. Bipolar was being mentioned behind my back and to my face at this point. I figured they must be right, if they are all seeing this. I started looking up Bipolar symptoms on my phone and thought maybe I could have Bipolar 2 Disorder or Generalized Anxiety Disorder. I was doubting my perceptions of reality and gaslighting myself, and I would do this for a couple years. This is not the way people get diagnosed with Bipolar. They usually get hospitalized for a severe manic episode, a severe depression, or get in trouble with the law. I knew it ran in families and I was at risk for having it since my older brother had it. I also had an identical twin who does not have any form of Bipolar. This is a very good indication that I most likely didn't either. I was about to be 34 and never had a severe mania or a severe depression, nor did I have extreme ups and downs in my life. I would later fall into every text book symptom of Post-Traumatic Stress Disorder (PTSD) or Complex Post-Traumatic Stress Disorder. At that moment I was suffering from an adjustment disorder, which involves PTSD like symptoms lasting six months or less. This was the official diagnosis I would receive. This was reality but you'll see how things got twisted and distorted.

I told my wife I wanted to go to my parent's house Easter morning. When we got to my parents' house, I started to feel a little better but was still breaking down crying at times. My sister mentioned that my older brother was crying like this too when he was manic. This was more gaslighting. My older brother had been hospitalized a few times for psychotic episodes of Bipolar and diagnosed while hospitalized as Bipolar 1 Disorder. He was arrested and then hospitalized after his first major episode. He was sleeping very little at night, drinking alcohol regularly, smoking marijuana, and abusing prescription pills like Adderall. He also blew through thousands of dollars going on an excessive spending spree. He had gone on many spending sprees prior to this point. He also had a trust fund with around $100k in it that he blew threw in his early 20's. He bought a lot of clothes that would sit with tags on them for years that he never wore. He also bought a brand-new Cadillac that he was driving off road during an episode of mania when he was 25. He would eventually get arrested for shooting a gun on private property where he was resisting arrest. My sister was so focused on using Bipolar language she learned from my older brother having it. She was working very hard to convince everyone, including me, that I was experiencing the same thing. The only issue with that is if anyone wanted to know my symptoms or how I was actually thinking or feeling, they could have asked me. Narcissists would rather tell you how you are thinking and feeling or let you know your thoughts and feelings are wrong. They are not interested in how you are actually thinking and feeling. Once again, I had no idea what I was dealing with, what a narcissist was at this time, or what was going to happen next. With my older brother when he was psychotic it was impossible to have a reasonable conversation with him, and he was never breaking down crying during his grandiose manic highs. He was on top of the world; he felt there was nothing wrong with him at these times. I'm not sure how she could compare what I was going through to his episodes. I knew I was suffering and I wanted relief from my stress. My mother and sister encouraged me to go to the Emergency Room (ER). I told them I didn't think much would change by going there. I already made contact with a mental health practice to be psychologically evaluated to get them off my back. I ended up agreeing to go to the Emergency Room (ER) that day. First, I went into a room by myself and explained what had been going on. They told me they could give me a Lorazepam, which is a Benzodiazepine for anxiety to calm me down, and I could go home. The other option was to go into an area where I could be seen by a Psychiatrist for a more thorough evaluation. I told them I want the most extensive psychological evaluation they could give me. So, I went into a locked unit where I had my own bed and there was one psychotic patient in there demanding to make a phone call and giving the staff a hard time. At that point in time it wasn't necessary for me to be evaluated but I felt I needed to do it to get an accurate answer for everyone else. I wanted to prove them wrong and that was my biggest problem. When you're dealing with a narcissist or a series of them, that's not a good idea. The best thing to do is to get away from them and not defend yourself, but I was in a war surrounded by them. I just wasn't aware of it. As I said, I had no idea what a narcissist was or what they were capable of up to this point.

I was accompanied by my wife, my sister, my mother, my twin brother, and my older brother. They all took turns coming in and sitting with me two people at a time. The Psychiatrist asked me a number of questions and I explained how I was overwhelmed and breaking down crying, which was not normal for me at all. We focused on all of the stressors I had going on in my life. My mom, sister, and wife all gave some input I was unaware of that I was "irrational" and "paranoid." I'm not really sure what else they told the Psychiatrist. I'm sure they told him they felt I was "manic." They really harped on having Bipolar in the family and a Schizophrenic aunt in the family. They were clearly attempting to manipulate the Psychiatrist at the ER that I had Bipolar Disorder when I reflect back. The Psychiatrist could find no signs of Bipolar in me that day. He encouraged me to identify my stressors and do my best to reduce them. There were many stressors as it was aside from the abuse, which none of us were aware was going on or how severe it was. From this day on one of them would always give the falsified Bipolar symptoms I wasn't suffering from in front of a Psychiatrist or Therapist. My mother would also make phone calls behind my back to give faulty input about my behavior and symptoms to manipulate any treating mental health professional. I continued to gaslight myself and believed I had a hypomanic episode of Bipolar Disorder, which is a milder form of the high you would see in a Bipolar patient. Looking back, it was pretty clear I was suffering from text book symptoms of an Adjustment

Disorder and Complex PTSD from being gaslit and abused. My ex-wife and sister were hoping I would be admitted to the Psych Department that day, but I was discharged after spending a few hours there.

CHAPTER 5

Bipolar or Psychological and Emotional Abuse?

In April 2016, I went into a mental health practice and began a psychological evaluation where I went over all my symptoms openly and honestly. The psychologist that did the intake said males tend to display depression as anger. She felt along with the psychiatrist I was assigned to that I was having an Adjustment Disorder, which used to be called a Situational Depression and put me on Lexapro. They had it right, but the answer wasn't good enough for my wife, my sister, and my mother. I had been staying with my parents a few nights, and said to my wife, "I think I should stay with them until we get the results of the psychological evaluation." I met with another Psychiatrist at this practice towards the end of April. Just like the Psychiatrist at the ER this Psychiatrist told me I needed to identify my stressors and triggers. I went to see my wife at the house we owned together on May 4 and explained what those stressors were. As I was explaining them to her, she grabbed my daughter, put her in the car, and drove her down to her brother's house. She has no empathy and couldn't even listen to what was stressing me out. I was sitting down when I was explaining this to her and didn't raise my voice. I brought up her spending, the house, and her parent's involvement in our marriage. She didn't want to listen to what I had to say. I realize now asking her to look at what she could do differently wasn't part of her personality. I was being stonewalled again and I couldn't take it anymore. The stonewalling and silent treatments were killing me. She could not take any accountability or responsibility nor could she compromise by having a healthy discussion. I had tried to reason with her too many times enough was enough, I grabbed all my clothes and anything I cared about at the time threw it in my truck and moved into my parents' house. The situation would get worse. My wife, my sister, and my mother came into my next appointment with the Psychiatrist on 17 May 2016. They told him I was irrational, paranoid, manic. etc. I looked at the Psychiatrist and shrugged my shoulders and said, "I don't know maybe." I said I would do whatever I had to do. They used Bipolar language and convinced the Psychiatrist I could be on the "Bipolar Spectrum" is how he worded it. At one point during this appointment it was just my wife and I speaking to the Psychiatrist. I talked about the conversation that took place with myself and her parents. She attempted to make me look crazy and said, "I wasn't there for that. They never said that. That never happened." At one point I became agitated and called her a "Spendaholic." The Psychiatrist was older and getting ready to retire. He was really nice, I liked him a lot. He started me on an atypical anti-psychotic medication called Latuda based on their input as well as my anger and frustration that day. He asked me if the Lexapro was helping, and I said no, the situation is getting worse. It didn't matter what medication I was on the situation was going to continue to get worse as you will see. Medication wasn't the issue in this case. I became severely depressed on this medication. I also developed restless leg syndrome from taking this medication, which was a potential side effect. My left leg was shaking uncontrollably many nights when trying to fall asleep. I was already suffering from Insomnia with all of the stress and anxiety. This medication wasn't helping me. He said to take Clonazepam at night with Latuda to assist with the side effects and sleeping. In the months I was on this medication, my wife said she would go to marriage counseling through the mental health practice, but she refused three appointments. She said, "You left, you don't get to decide when you come back." She also said, "You abandoned me and your daughter." She claimed that I needed an individual therapist through the mental health practice. I agreed to this and started therapy there. The therapist described my ex-wife as toxic and narcissistic. She also mentioned that we needed to attempt to work things out in marriage counseling. My ex-wife told me that her friend from college was a Social Worker and more qualified to be a Therapist compared to the individual Therapist assigned to me. I was begging her to go to marriage counseling and to think about our daughter. I gave her numerous opportunities to work things out. I was getting frustrated and threatening divorce in July 2016. Instead she served divorce papers the first week of August 2016 at the same time another marriage counseling session was scheduled and I was still optimistic that she would go. I felt she was as committed as I was to the marriage and would do anything to work things out. She would later laugh that she went to the most aggressive pit bull lawyer in central Connecticut shortly after the psychiatrist appointment in May and had a consultation with her to block me from using her. She also inquired about getting a restraining order put on me. She wanted to paint the picture that I was mentally ill and could be dangerous. Every move she made was very cold and calculated. I was devastated and depressed trying to accept the divorce and figure out what was going on. I felt like a complete failure and that everything was my fault. I felt I was losing my family and the fact that I had Bipolar Disorder was the reason for it. This is what I was telling myself. I was breaking down and crying many days in my office in July and August during my school's summer program. I would pull myself together to teach my classes, but it was a struggle. I also had to complete my comprehensive exam for my master's program and I accomplished that. My daughter had been staying with me overnight on some week nights and weekend nights at my parent's house before the divorce papers were served. In the divorce papers, it said nothing was supposed to change, but she wouldn't allow my daughter to sleep over anymore after the divorce papers were served in August 2016. I was used to putting my daughter to bed every night prior to leaving the house except for the Wednesday nights she would stay with my mom when I had class so this was a major change I wasn't prepared for. She was filing for sole custody and using my "mental illness" as the reason. I didn't want any confrontation so I passed my daughter off to my wife and her mother who would pull into my parents' driveway together. It felt like they were holding her hostage from me. Having her ripped away and never in the room next to me was killing me. I would make calls to speak to our daughter, but my wife wouldn't answer the phone. I was the saddest and most depressed I had ever been. They would do this for six months not allowing me to have an overnight with my daughter. My wife told family relations at the Courthouse that she was not agreeing to sleepovers. The Mediator said, "He's the father he's going to get sleepovers." She told the Mediator that she "disagreed." Narcissists have a personality that is low in agreeableness and anytime we would meet with a Co-parenting Counselor in the near future there were many times she would say "I disagree" to any reasonable request I would make. My mental health was deteriorating with PTSD symptoms getting worse as time went on and that's what she wanted so she could go after sole custody. I'm not sure how a Mediator at the Court house, lawyers we were paying $350-400 an hour, and the State of Connecticut can allow a parent to walk out of the Court house with a temporary custody agreement giving one parent Wednesday nights for three hours and every other weekend with no sleepovers. This was the time I would spend with my daughter from the beginning of August to 23 January 2017, which felt like a hostage situation and an eternity. My mental health would slowly deteriorate with me sinking deeper and deeper into depression with every day that went by. This agreement that gave me hardly anytime with our daughter was a traumatic experience by itself never mind everything else that was going on.

At the mental health practice, my case got transferred to the Chairman of Psychiatry, and on 26 July 2016, he told me it was highly unlikely that I had Bipolar Disorder even though I had an older brother that had Bipolar 1 Disorder. This was a relief. My loving and caring sister or so I thought got wind of this and wanted to come to my next appointment. I didn't think anything of it so I said sure. On 23 August 2016, she told the Psychiatrist she felt I was paranoid towards her even though I clearly had trust issues with her after she went behind my back with my wife to marriage counseling. I'm not sure how you could be paranoid towards one person. I started paying attention to her back stabbing behavior. Looking back, I believe that is what she was referring to anytime she would call me paranoid. She went on to talk about a family friend we knew that got diagnosed in her 50's and how you can get diagnosed later in life. She was a saleswoman of Bipolar that day and the Psychiatrist bought it. The manipulation and gaslighting continued. There was no way to know she would do this, but once I figured it out, I knew she would never be with me in front of any mental health professional ever again. It took way too long for me to figure it out, but better late than never. The Bipolar diagnosis was very damaging to me psychologically. Accepting a severe mental illness at a time when your marriage is falling apart and your wife is attempting to sever the relationship you have with your child is devastating. It was now a part of my medical record that could be subpoenaed at Court for the custody case. This certainly wasn't going to help my case.

Eventually, my therapist mentioned to me that my experience sounded like Munchausen Syndrome by Proxy or Factitious Disorder Imposed on Another. With this disorder the person lying and exaggerating medical symptoms is usually a mother that is a primary caregiver to a child, but it could also be a father. My case is very interesting because in this instance it was my younger sister and we are both adults. This usually happens when that caregiver has borderline, antisocial, or narcissistic personality disorder. My mother, sister, and wife were all lying and exaggerating mental health symptoms in front of numerous mental health professionals at this point. I'm thankful I was eventually able to figure all of this out, but at the time, I had no idea what was going on. After the appointment with the Chairman of Psychiatry and my sister, my anxiety was through the roof and I fell into a severe depression rather quickly after the misdiagnosis. My thoughts really were racing now with anxiety. I was in a bad place. I just got served divorce papers three weeks prior, my daughter is basically being held hostage from me, and now I'm being told I have Bipolar 1 Disorder. I thought I was mentally ill, worthless, and that bipolar was completely to blame for all of the issues taking place. This type of gaslighting could severely depress anyone. One of the things I had going for me was that I completed my master's program with a 3.96 GPA in July 2016 – Not bad for someone that was being made out to be severely mentally ill. I was beginning to think I was not worthy of living and giving up on life. I felt like I was losing everything. My daughter was everything to me and I was hardly in her life at this point. My wife was stacking things against me to limit my time with our daughter as much as she could.

I was mentally exhausted from questioning my sanity. I had obsessive, intrusive thoughts, and kept ruminating about the situation. Thoughts continued to play over and over in my mind more quickly. I was shaking with anxiety before bed with my daughter continuing to be kept from me. My daughter also had a difficult time with this. She would kick and scream when she left to go back to my wife because she didn't want to leave me. She also wet the bed during and after the divorce process. This was a text book sign of trauma in a child.

My whole body was in pain. My neck and back were really tight and stiff. I didn't have much of an appetite. This was in October 2016, two months after the divorce papers were served. I was severely depressed. I called the Chairman of Psychiatry for an emergency appointment and checked myself into an Intensive Outpatient Program I started in November. My employer was very supportive and I went on Family Medical Leave of Absence for six weeks. I was going to attend a Partial Hospital Program and Intensive Outpatient Program through the hospital where the mental health practice was. My employer knew the situation and that I was having a really hard time functioning at work. I came off Latuda and started a low dose of Seroquel, which is a jack of all trades drug for Bipolar Depression, Generalized Anxiety Disorder, Major Depressive Disorder, and PTSD as an off-label use. I was suffering from severe anxiety and severe depression symptoms. It was a good temporary fix because I needed something that would knock me out so I could sleep and not think about what was happening. Seroquel is a very sedating medication. Prior to taking it, I was getting a broken six or seven hours of sleep. The most severe depression symptoms lasted about five months roughly the same amount of time my daughter was being kept away from me. I had to start rebuilding my self-esteem, which was down to nothing. While in the program I was anxious, depressed, had difficulty falling asleep and staying asleep, intrusive thoughts, was dissociating, and felt disconnected. These are all of the symptoms a victim of severe gaslighting and emotional abuse would suffer from according to Dr. George Simon, a leading expert on disturbed manipulative people. Overall, I felt numb and paralyzed. The six-foot-three-inch athletic guy that was 190 lbs. for the past fifteen years give or take 5 lbs., had a lot of friends, a pitcher on a national championship baseball team in college, and captain of most sports teams growing up was 172 lbs. I was on psychological and emotional life support. I lost about 20 pounds. If you want to psychologically and emotionally torture someone make them believe they have a mental illness they don't have and keep their child away from them that will do it.

In the Intensive Outpatient Program, I talked about getting healthy to be there for my daughter. I participated in every group therapy and applied myself every day. I never thought to myself I wasn't like these people or didn't need to be there. This is how my older brother described his group therapy experiences. I knew I needed help. There was a daily check in board where we rated our sleep, anxiety and depression each day, and mentioned a goal we had for the day. The board also had written on it one minute at a time, one hour at a time, and one day at a time on it. When I first got there, I was focusing on getting from one minute to the next because I was so dissociated and my brain was attempting to numb out the situation. It was a struggle to see one minute to the next. I dreaded free time and the weekends. Looking back this is probably because my mother and sister were the people I was around the most. I felt safest when I was there in the program and actually looked forward to pushing myself to go each day, but I felt like a zombie most days just going through the motions. They increased my Seroquel to 300mg while I was in the program and put me on the extended release form of it. This made me feel like even more of a zombie. I was sleeping about ten or eleven hours each night. I was overmedicated at this point. While in the program I could relate to a man that was suffering from a major depressive episode, he had Major Depressive Disorder and I seemed to be in a similar mental state. I could also relate to a woman who had PTSD. There was a man with Bipolar who really did appear manic, a Schizophrenic man, and a guy younger than me with Generalized Anxiety Disorder. I noticed clear differences in these guys that didn't seem to apply to what I had been through or what I was going through. We were all in a dog fight together when we were there pulling in the same direction to get our lives back on track and get to a better place. These people were really supportive when I said I wanted to get healthy to be able to spend more time with my daughter, they knew that meant everything to me. My sister only came around to see how much pain and suffering I was in. She knew I was down and wanted to do anything in her power to keep me there except I didn't realize it at the time. At the Intensive Outpatient Program, a different Psychiatrist was assigned to me. My mom and sister wanted to come in and talk to him to give input about how I was doing. I let them speak to the Psychiatrist and they explained how they felt I wasn't getting better even though my depression actually was getting better. They gave their usual manipulation spiel of me being Bipolar, angry, and irrational etc. After they got done talking to him, he was thinking about adding Lithium to the Seroquel; my anxiety went way up again. Lithium is a mood stabilizer that has been used to treat Bipolar for a long time with some really rough side effects. Thankfully he didn't end up doing this since it was unnecessary, but the gaslighting was getting worse from them and it was clear that it was never going to stop. Every time my mother or sister would talk to a Psychiatrist, they looked at me like I was doing much worse than I actually was. My sister kept saying she was just trying to "help" me.

I would eventually learn from Meredith Miller an expert in the field of narcissistic abuse and healing that female narcissists will say that they are just "concerned" and want to "help" you but that is code that they are going to smear and abuse you. I believe she is right about this. My mother, my sister, and my ex-wife had me right where they wanted me is what it felt like. I was in the inferior vulnerable position and they were in the superior controlling position. Right where narcissists, sociopaths, or psychopaths want their victims, nothing gets better than that for them. They take sadistic pleasure in being in the powerful superior position and seeing someone suffer. They were like a pack of Wolves smelling blood on an injured defenseless Deer out in the wild. Of course those Wolves are going to rip that Deer apart until there is nothing left of it. Narcissists do the same thing when a human being is vulnerable and struggling. Like Wolves or a Shark, they smell blood and attack. It's inhumane especially when your claiming to love the person you are abusing. It was interesting that when I got better and was doing well my sister never came around or wanted to see me. It felt like she was upset I bounced back fairly quickly considering the circumstances. My depression and anxiety symptoms would go from severe, to moderate, to mild, to gone slowly over a span of three and a half years. Many factors contribute to a person's recovery time. The less that ties you to one of the abusers the quicker you can recover when you're doing everything right to get out of the relationship. In my case when I left my wife's house I went straight to my family for support where my mother and sister were the people that wanted to be involved the most. It was kind of like running out of one burning building and going to another building for safety only to realize that building is also on fire. Rather than pour water on me to put the fire out, my mother and sister were basically pouring gasoline on me; the only way to stop it was to get away from them. I would eventually realize there was no other option. I would estimate the healing and recovery time from a prolonged toxic relationship is between one to two years once you have no contact or very limited contact.

My wife pushed for supervised visits for a short amount of time with my daughter while I was in the program. The Co-parenting Counselor we were working with agreed my wife would be the supervisor for the visits. It felt like the grim reaper was hovering over me as I played on the carpet in the playroom with my daughter for about thirty minutes to an hour when we would set up visits at my parents' house. The co-parenting meetings prior to me entering the Intensive Outpatient Program were torture; she was using the Counselor to abuse me and make me out to be an incompetent father. My wife claimed our daughter was allergic to dogs and was coming home with a rash on her butt because I was irresponsible and allowing her to be around the dogs. I would later have my daughter tested for allergies and there was no pet allergy. In the meetings, she would throw out false accusation after false accusation. I felt like I was always defending myself. I met my wife and my daughter out for breakfast one morning while in the program. I was shocked that she invited me out and she asked me what it feels like in reference to the depression. I said, "I feel numb and paralyzed." She told me her cousin's wife's first husband has Bipolar, he's in jail, and the medications don't really work." She was basically telling me just give up now and kill yourself because there is no hope for you.

Up until that day I was holding onto to some type of hope that we would work things out. I was thinking about the life we had together and how we had a beautiful daughter together. In my mind I thought I would go home to her, take my medication and everything would be ok but she never made any effort towards that outcome. Thank god that didn't happen. From that day on I knew that hope was gone. I could feel she wanted me dead. This was rock bottom of toxic relationships for me when I reflect back. It was at this moment I fully accepted that the marriage was over.

At this point I didn't really trust anyone. I realized what my mother and sister had been saying was not helping me at all. I was completely isolated. This is where a malignant narcissist, sociopath, or psychopath wants their victims. I was dependent on my mother and sister to tell me what my reality was. This was a very dangerous place to be. I was suffering psychologically and emotionally. I felt like I was being suffocated. A narcissist wants to isolate you and take away any person that can support you. They want you to have nobody to turn to or trust, which is an effort to bring you back to them and depend on them. This is where I was begging and pleading with my mother, sister, and wife trying to get their approval. My thoughts and feelings continued to be ignored, or everything was turned around on me. I would eventually learn this was never going to change. I was lucky to have my identical twin as a support person, but it was still a struggle. He had to helplessly watch me suffer; there wasn't much he could do, but I do appreciate that he was there for support when he could be. I graduated from the Intensive Outpatient Program and returned to work just before Christmas break in 2016. I had experienced a lot of dissociative symptoms that made it difficult to concentrate at work prior to entering the program and those symptoms were finally starting to dissipate but it was still a struggle. When I got out of the Intensive Outpatient Program, I questioned the Chairman of Psychiatry and he said he had a lot of doubt about the diagnosis. He also said, "I'm not going back on the diagnosis." "Once you receive this diagnosis, it's very hard to get it to go away," is what he told me. I believe he kept the diagnosis because it would reflect poorly on him to go back on it. He appeared to have a big ego having the title of Chairman of Psychiatry. He didn't seem like a guy that wanted to admit he made a mistake. He would say things like there is no blood test for Bipolar Disorder. He flip-flopped back and forth on the diagnosis, which showed he really had no idea. I was still battling through moderate depression after the New Year. Within three weeks we signed a custody agreement that gave me Wednesday nights and every other weekend with overnights on 23 January 2017. After what I just came out of, I signed the agreement so I could have the visitation with overnights. If I didn't sign it, I knew I could be punished at any time and visitation could be withheld from me. I didn't want to have my wife be in control and change the rules of visitation, if I did something to upset her. I always knew one day when I was in a better place I would push for more time with our daughter. I was very confused and somewhat believed I had some form of Bipolar and was still talking myself into a Bipolar 2 diagnosis. I continued to gaslight myself and doubt myself due to what appeared to be gaslighting from the Chairman of Psychiatry when I reflect back. It's shocking that you go somewhere for help and get psychologically and emotionally messed with. In his defense based on my sister's input there really was no other diagnosis he could have come up with. A part of me didn't believe the distorted reality that had been created for me but part of me did. The first week of February 2017, I moved into a three-bedroom apartment that I rented. I knew I had to get out of my parent's house. Being in that environment wasn't healthy for my recovery. I still hadn't put it together that my mother had a very harmful Cluster B personality disorder. I just felt stuck like I was in quick sand living there and going nowhere. I was making progress but was getting frustrated at how slow my progress was. Healing is a slow process coming out of these relationships and I wasn't out yet. I was still confused about what had happened to me and continuing to happen to me. A narcissist wants to keep their victims disoriented and off balance. It was a team effort by my wife, her parents, my mother, and my sister. They were still taking shots at me to manipulate and control me any chance they got.

I had conversations with my mother that went nowhere and just went around and around in circles saying the same things.

One day during my severe depression I expressed my thoughts and feelings to her. I was looking to her for support and she called me "selfish" and "paranoid." There have been countless times where my siblings, and my father had been called selfish assholes by her. Most conversations ended with "your wrong." The take home message always was your thoughts and feelings are wrong so don't bother sharing them. She was so good at making you feel worthless and knocking your self-esteem down very quickly. That's how it felt anyway. My thoughts and feelings have not once been validated by my mother. I finally came to this realization in therapy and it makes sense that narcissists are not capable of validating your feelings. After this whole experience, the therapist I originally went to took me through cognitive processing therapy, which is a step by step manual to overcoming trauma and PTSD. I was able to identify stuck points that were preventing me from letting go of past situations so I could look at them differently. Many of these stuck points were part of my programming developed in childhood. The majority of conversations where I went to my mother looking for support would end up with my mom blaming my father for everything that went wrong in her life and bad mouthing him. When I was living at my parents house my dad said to me, "I get badgered and belittled every day." I know now this is all projection, blame shifting, learned behavior, and unresolved issues she has with her narcissistic father. If you have a narcissistic parent, chances are they had one too. If you look closely enough once you know what to look for, it's easy to identify.

CHAPTER 6

Finally Divorced

On 7 September 2017, we finally got divorced. After signing the custody agreement that gave me Wednesday nights and every other weekend in January of 2017, the actual divorce was dragged on another nine months. This was mainly due to the financial part of the divorce; my wife was figuring out how she could extract the most money out of me. In April of 2017, my father and I were subpoenaed to have our depositions taken at my wife's lawyer's office. When the time came for the depositions, my wife only wanted to take my father's deposition. During the deposition they put all of my financial statements in front of my father and asked him questions about them. For example, there was one annuity that he set up for me in 1983 a year after I was born and they asked him when he set it up for me. Then they put the trust fund in front of him and asked him the reason he and my grandfather set the trust fund up for me. Then they asked him if he had any other financial accounts that may have had both of our names on it. I sent a frustrated email about the deposition to my wife afterward. She said, "We had to take one of your depositions because you didn't give us all of your financial statements." That was an interesting response since they put all of my financial statements in front of my father the day he was deposed. She wasn't entitled to any portion of them because our marriage was so short meaning the depositions were a complete waste of time and money. It told me a lot about her character and who she was. She was after the roughly $200,000 in annuities and investments that I had behind me, which was true right from the start. Like I mentioned before she felt she was entitled to anything and everything I had. I also believe she was looking for a way to get her hands on the portion of the few million dollars my father had, which is why he was deposed that day. He told me he felt sick after that experience and that he felt my wife's lawyer was just as bad as she was.

Starting on 7 September 2017, we were scheduled for a two-day trial to get divorced. If we got divorced on the 8th it would have been our 5th year wedding anniversary. We went in on the first day of the trial, my mother and sister wanted to be there with me and I foolishly allowed them to be there. It's clear that they wanted to be a part of any drama. They get a rush from situations that the average person would do anything to avoid.

For example, the high conflict divorce we were currently involved with. This was exciting to all of them except for me I had wanted to get it over with and have more time with our daughter for over a year at this point. My wife's parents were there with her. The main goal that day for them was to give me nothing as far as money and possessions that needed to be divided. There were many possessions I let go of. Two of them I asked for were a fairly new lawn mower and my snow blower. Even though her or her parents were paying someone to remove snow and mow the lawn, she refused to let these items go. I knew it was best to just let all furniture and possessions go and cut my losses so that's what I did. The house was going to her and even though I put $43,000 into real estate and her parents $56,000, I didn't want any money. I just wanted more time with our daughter. I offered 50/50 physical custody and I wouldn't take any money. They didn't go for that. I didn't want to touch any of the money that my wife's parents gave to us. If they had to pay me out for the house and possessions, my lawyer calculated it would have been $50,000. I offered for them to pay me $25,000 and wanted more time with our daughter. We ended up settling on $15,000, and I got a little more time with our daughter. On Thursday nights, when it wouldn't be my weekend, I would have dinner with her for three hours. Then on Monday nights, after it wasn't my weekend, I would have dinner with her for a few hours. At first, they wouldn't budge with any additional time; my wife's father intimidated my lawyer by saying, "He's Bipolar." We would eventually settle on the additional dinner times. My lawyer was afraid to go into the Courtroom that day and go in front of a judge. The misdiagnosis definitely played a huge role in my lawyer and myself feeling it would have a negative impact on custody. She was a nice woman but was a collaborative divorce lawyer and not built for what we were up against. My lawyer said, "You'll meet a nice girl one day, and custody is modifiable forever." This didn't make me feel any better that my daughter and I were getting screwed out of time together and were both traumatized. I didn't know we were in a high conflict divorce nor did I know anything about high conflict personalities. I did my research so I would be prepared with a high conflict lawyer when I would eventually go for modifying custody in an attempt to get my daughter the time she deserved with both of us.

CHAPTER 7

Not My Reality

In January 2018, I questioned the Chairman of Psychiatry for the last time about the Bipolar diagnosis. I said, "You have no basis for this diagnosis with the absence of a severe mania. Without a severe mania my entire life (I was 35 years old at this time) there is no way I could possibly have Bipolar 1 Disorder, this isn't my reality."

In visits prior to this I told him my mother and sister are not helping me. He had met both of them and made the diagnosis based on their input.

He would say things like, "Michael do you feel people are out to get you?"

"Michael this isn't going well for you. I think we should increase your medication."

I was at the point where I felt I was being gaslighted by the Chairman of Psychiatry. I knew I finally had to get the hell out of there and get another opinion.

My twin brother came to one appointment with me and met him. Again, I feel it's important to note that my identical twin doesn't have any form of Bipolar Disorder and that's a very good indication that I wouldn't have it either. After that appointment, my brother said, "You have to get away from that guy and get another opinion." So, I did.

The chairman agreed it was no longer appropriate for him to treat me. At this point I had done enough research on Cluster B personality disorders and realized that I had been duped into believing I was Bipolar. I had begun to research information on narcissism and came across a YouTube video by Ross Rosenberg titled, "Unmasking the Covert Narcissist." He also had a good video on gaslighting. After watching these videos, I could clearly see that my mother, my sister, my ex-wife, her mother, and her father were saying word for word what Ross Rosenberg was describing a narcissist would say to gaslight you and make you question your sanity. I finally knew enough to keep my mom and sister away from psychiatrists and therapists moving forward.

In March of 2018, I went to another mental health practice in central Connecticut and explained how I felt I could possibly have Bipolar Disorder and received this diagnosis from the other mental health practice. The Psychologist that did my intake was very confused. When the Psychiatric Nurse met me, she said, "Why do you think you have Bipolar Disorder?" She said, "I don't think your Bipolar."

I said, "Bipolar 1 is written all over my psychological evaluation."

She asked me to get a copy of my psychological evaluation from the other mental health practice and bring it to her.

She read through the entire file, which was almost two years' worth of information. I questioned my sanity for a year and eleven months up to that point.

She said, "You're not Bipolar. I just think you were overwhelmed."

She was right, that's exactly how I felt the entire time. I didn't have to question my sanity anymore. She wanted to get me off the 150 mg of Seroquel I was on and put me on something else. We decided on Trazadone. I had done a lot of research on medications and for the symptoms I was experiencing, I agreed that this sounded like a good medication. It is a sedating antidepressant, and for the next year, my psychological and emotional health would improve tremendously. In her opinion I was back to having a chronic Adjustment Disorder or Complex PTSD symptoms.

The first psychiatrist had it right without the manipulators present. I wasn't crazy once again. What was interesting is my father is currently on the same medication and takes a dose of 100 mg of Trazadone. We both had in common we suffered narcissistic abuse, there is no doubt about it, the only difference is he had no idea why he was on the medication. He was a workaholic that was his way of coping with being married to my mother. He had taken so much abuse and was so conditioned to it. My twin brother and I joked with him because we always caught him watching lifetime movies. We asked him if he could relate the lifetime movies to his personal life. When my twin brother and I asked him to describe our mother, he mentioned two words, "fatal attraction." The movie *Fatal Attraction* was based on a borderline woman, although this movie took it to an extreme it's not too far off. I think he actually enjoyed the dysfunctional relationship; he would laugh about it like it was a game to him. His marriage was just like a lifetime movie, there would be no happy ending. He told me he wouldn't get a divorce because it would be too costly.

CHAPTER 8

High Conflict Lawyer

In November of 2018, I met with a high conflict lawyer that I was referred to from a friend I knew through playing Baseball.

When I had a consultation with him, he said, "I only do high conflict."

When I described my ex-wife, he said, "She's the type if she could get rid of you, she would."

I replied, "No doubt about it."

I had a lot of documentation to show him. It is important to document anything you can with proof. For example, phone calls made that were not answered, emails, and text messages with the dates in order. I had numerous texts and emails asking to see our daughter on days my ex-wife was not available and I was free to take care of her. She would have her mom take care of her on those days. This went on for years. I had documentation for every time that happened. We came up with a plan to modify custody so my daughter would have a plan with less transitions and more stability. We sent a letter to my ex-wife that would give me 45 percent of the time and her 55 percent of the time to try to stay out of Court. She didn't respond to the letter. I told him she wasn't going to agree to anything we proposed. He mentioned maybe we could meet and try to mediate. He also mentioned that he had a good working relationship with her lawyer. This is exactly what my first lawyer told me. I told him I would go if he could set up a mediation meeting, but if I was right about her having the personality disorder, I thought she had, there was no chance that was going to happen. In our agreement we had to attempt to work things out in co-parenting prior to returning to Court. I sent an email to my ex-wife and the Co-parenting Counselor letting her know I wanted to discuss modifications to the parenting plan that would give our daughter more stability. We set up a meeting and my ex-wife refused. I attempted to set up another meeting and again she refused. I took all the proper steps prior to returning to Court. We filed a motion to modify custody after the New Year in 2019. We didn't get to Court until 22 April 2019. At Court that day I showed little to no emotion. My ex-wife was there with her mother who looked at me shaking her head in disgust. My ex-wife made many false accusations that day.

She said, "He's insane. He encourages our daughter to sleep in the bed with him. He keyed his sister's car. He hands out pamphlets on narcissism. The Co-parenting Counselor refused to work with him because of his behavior."

None of these accusations were true.

My lawyer said to her lawyer, "Your client looks a little crazy."

The goal that day was to get a custody evaluator appointed to psychologically evaluate both of us. This would protect me from the false accusations of mental illness I continued to face and allow her to reveal who she really was. She said she would agree to the evaluation, if I paid for it. These evaluations aren't cheap they cost $10,000. I knew this it what was needed to expose her and protect our daughter. We came to an agreement that I would pay for 70 percent of it.

I also filed a motion for a Therapist for our daughter and got one appointed. There were many inappropriate comments my daughter made to me that she was hearing from my ex-wife. The worst one was, "Mommy technically wants you to get sick so she can have all the time with me ever since I said I want more time with you." It was a really sad situation my daughter would say things like, "I feel like mommy froze my heart." I also heard, "Mommy says you lie all the time." She also said, "Mommy said daddy's house isn't my real house." There is much more but I won't get into it.

My ex-wife claimed our daughter didn't need a Therapist because she was doing well in school. Once my daughter opened up in therapy, it was clear to the Child Psychologist that she needed therapy.

I'm thankful I was able to step up and do the right thing at the right time for her.

CHAPTER 9

The Importance of the Share Nothing Plan

On Monday, 13 May 2019, the Court appointed a Custody Evaluator to evaluate me and my ex-wife. This was the chance for my experience to be validated along with exposing the Bipolar diagnosis given to me as complete bullshit. The answer I got from the most recent psychological evaluation in regard to my mental health symptoms again wasn't good enough for my mother, my sister, or my ex-wife. They were all still subscribing to the reality that I was Bipolar. I could sense my mom, sister, and my ex-wife scrambling to see if they could keep the lie going. I've heard most Cluster B's are manipulative enough to get through a psychological evaluation without anyone being able to pick up on them having a personality disorder. Would my ex-wife sneak through a full custody and psychological evaluation that entailed a number of personality tests? Either way my main focus was to get the time my daughter deserves with me through this process and get the custody plan that was best for her. I was also ready to break free of this alternate reality they all created for me and I was already well on my way.

On 9 May 2019, my mother, my sister, and her husband who also was subscribing to the Bipolar reality were deposed by my ex-wife. They were interrogated for any information to make me look bad. My mother had discussed text message disagreements between us with my ex-wife. My ex-wife subpoenaed and obtained over 800 pages of text messages dating back to our divorce date of 7 September 2017. The text messages she subpoenaed were between me and my mother, me and my sister, and me and my sister's husband. I didn't know it was possible to subpoena text messages like this unless there was a murder investigation, but this was really happening. They had to get their own lawyer to represent them; it was clear they didn't have my back. Prior to this happening I had a feeling if we were to go to a trial my mother and sister would be sitting with my ex-wife hand picking text messages to make me look bad. The custody evaluation was basically the trial where the decision for custody would be based off of. Exactly what I expected would happen was happening. The first thing my mother told the lawyer that was representing her was that I was Bipolar. Her lawyer called my lawyer to ask about this. My lawyer then called me and questioned me about me being Bipolar. I had just given him my medical records from both mental health practices, which explained the reasons I wasn't Bipolar. My lawyer believed my mother was on my side at first, I explained to him that she was not prior to this. At this point he could clearly see she wasn't. I attempted to explain to my mother what the mental health professionals at the most recent mental health practice had told me after I got the results from that psychological evaluation. She tried to call them behind my back to distort reality, telling them she was concerned about me, and I was suspicious of others, but they didn't buy into her manipulations. Suspicious was just another word for paranoid. Nothing had changed from when this all started back in March 2016. The Psychiatric Nurse called me during my lunch break at work to ask if I was doing ok after receiving a phone call from my mother. I let her know everything was ok and went back to work. Unlike the other mental health practice, she didn't take what my mother said as my reality. She thoroughly evaluated me and the situation unlike the Chairman of Psychiatry. My mother, my sister along with her husband, and my ex-wife were all working together and the lawyers along with the Custody Evaluator and Child Psychologist figured that out very quickly. My mother would say things like, "I'm concerned about your irrational texts." This was more gaslighting. In one argument with her, she said,

"You're going to see what's going to happen with Marie because of your irrational texts." Meaning she felt I was going to lose time with my daughter because of the text messages and she wanted to be a part of that happening. It was clear to me she wanted to sabotage and undermine my attempts at getting more time with my daughter. That's the narcissistic mother for you right there. I had sent hundreds of back and forth text messages between me and my mother in confidence in regard to how I felt my ex-wife was a narcissist. I texted the reasons why with online articles and screen shots texted to her to back it up. This was me attempting to explain to my narcissist mother that my ex-wife was a narcissist. This is a behavior that I engaged in too many times and was getting me nowhere. The definition of insanity is engaging in the same behavior over and over again expecting different results. I needed to change my behavior. The best advice I can give is stop trying to reason and prove your point to a narcissist; you'll end up feeling defeated every time. They will never "agree" with you regardless of how right you are and how wrong they are.

The same abuse had been going on for over three years now and I was prepared for it this time. The only way to stop it was to stop texting along with cutting off all communication with them until the Court proceedings were over. So that's what I did, which proved to be the best decision I could have made for my case and sanity. With a narcissist it's imperative you share nothing, not a damn thing. The best thing to do is to not try to prove your point. My sister's husband had now become a flying monkey or a puppet, as my twin brother called him, for my ex-wife and my sister. Puppet was fitting because he did anything and everything my sister asked him to do. It was like a ventriloquist act with my sister and her husband. She told him what to do and say and he complied. I've heard the term flying monkey before regarding narcissistic abuse. It's also called abuse by proxy. This is the person the narcissist sends to do their bidding in an attempt to achieve their agenda. If my sister could manipulate and brainwash me into believing I had Bipolar Disorder, I don't blame him for subscribing to that reality. My sister was very deceptive and manipulative. Plus if you cross her and disagree with her, you'll be on the receiving end of her wrath and rage. She put him up to texting me and my twin brother that I was "paranoid" and he wanted to get me in front of a mental health professional. I let him know I wasn't going to entertain accusations of make-believe paranoia anymore. What all of them didn't know is that I had a copy of my medical records that had weekly therapy notes stating I had no paranoia and no delusions dating all the way back to March 2016. I told him I would talk to him or my sister one on one and that therapy wouldn't be effective in my opinion. This is what my sister wanted and got him to attempt to round us up for family therapy for more abuse. These text messages were also subpoenaed by my ex-wife and presented to the Custody Evaluator. I clearly wasn't paranoid. My sister was behind making me out to be mentally ill and the problem just like my ex-wife for a long time. I was in a completely different place with no depression and much less anxiety this time. I saw my sister for who she was – A very sneaky abuser.

My twin brother called my sister at one point and said, "Could you say something positive to Michael? Look at what he went through, then he went out and got a better teaching job."

When my brother asked that question, she said, "How dare you say that to me. I did everything for that fucking kid." She was talking about me like she was my mother, like she raised me.

My sister also began yelling at my twin brother saying, "You're just agreeing with him, stop agreeing with him."

My twin brother became frustrated with her and said, "I'm not agreeing with you right now." My twin brother said he had pretty much cut my sister out of his life for years now and he was distancing himself from our mother as well.

Regarding my sisters' comment, I was unaware that rewriting my history with lies, rumors, and false accusations, along with creating an alternate reality for me where I had a severe mental illness with my ex-wife behind my back was doing everything for me. In her eyes I'm supposed to accept this reality, thank her, and apologize to her because she was the victim of this situation. She has no insight as to how much harm she had caused me. According to her and my mother, they were victims because I stood up for myself. WTF, which stands for "What the fuck?"

My sister inflicted a tremendous amount of psychological and emotional pain without any regard for my feelings. She had no empathy, no remorse, no guilt but she was very good at getting people to believe she was a loving, caring sister that was just concerned and wanted to help me. Holy mind fuck moment. How could a person torture and torment another human being in an inhumane manner and play the victim? Narcissists love to play the victim. I was caught up in what type of narcissist she was for a long time. Does she have a dark triad personality? Is she a covert narcissist, malignant narcissist, a borderline, socio-pathic or psychopathic? It doesn't matter what the label is. It was evident that she had a harmful Cluster B personality disorder. Overthinking exactly how many crossover traits she had wasn't productive. I was clearly seeing the amount of damage that was done to me and the potential harm that could continue to be done, if I didn't cut her out of my life, was not measurable.

When confronted about the situation she can never answer a question. She just says, "I'm not talking about this." This is another example of text book stonewalling. I gave her and my mother numerous opportunities to do the right thing and they made the choice to abuse me. They were always evasive and wouldn't talk to me about anything I was upset about when I asked to speak to them one on one. They were very comfortable aligning others against me to gang up on me. The last text my sister ever sent me before I blocked her number was in January of 2018 in regards to how long it took my older brother to come to terms with his Bipolar and that she thought I was going through the same thing. By that time, I figured out she was a narcissist and had been gaslighting and smearing me for almost two years. I couldn't listen to it anymore.

The other interesting thing my twin and I noticed about my mother and sister is that neither one of them congratulated either one of us on getting better teaching jobs in August of 2018. My twin brother took a better teaching job that was a great opportunity for him and I happened to do the same thing for the 2018-19 school year. My mother never once said she was proud of either one of us. They were always there to tell you what was wrong with you, abuse you, and remind you of your shortcomings, but never there to celebrate your successes. That's narcissism. If they could ruin anything good you have going for you, they were right there ready to do that. It's a really sick disorder. They repeatedly said that they were just "concerned" about me and that they just wanted to "help" me. They are insinuating that you are the problem when they say this. What they are essentially saying is that there is a problem and you are that problem, when you accept that you are the problem and do as we say then everything will be fine. If you comply with their demands, then all of sudden there is nothing wrong with you. They want you to conform to their way of life. My ex-wife and her parents are the same way. The only thing a narcissist is "concerned" about is losing power and control over you. That was the main "concern" for my mother. When I reviewed the text message exchanges between me and my mother, I found the word concern in there at least 50 times. There was next to nothing for her to be concerned about with me at the time of these texts.

CHAPTER 10

Family Therapy

My sister wanted to go to a Family Therapist with our entire family, but first she went with her husband to distort reality and try to manipulate the Therapist. This wasn't much different than attempting marriage counseling with my ex-wife behind my back. They won't face you one on one with a Therapist. They either have to bring other people in, which is called triangulation, or use the Therapist to abuse you, which is also an example of triangulation. Using the Therapist to abuse you is just a game to them. If they can manipulate the Therapist, they will keep going. If not, then they won't go anymore. They will say the Therapist is not competent and suggest another Therapist. I read this in articles and experienced it firsthand. Therapy is a manipulation game to them that you don't want to play. My sister wouldn't go one on one with my twin brother either.

My twin brother and I went together as well to this Family Therapist who was optimistic that we would work things out in therapy. She was a really nice woman that had no idea how dysfunctional our family dynamic was. The Therapist said our sister was "genuinely concerned" about Michael. I brought this up to the Therapist I was seeing and he got really upset saying, "Genuinely concerned my ass." This phrase, which was complete bullshit, happened to pop up again. It seems to be a common phrase that covert abusers use. The concern was based on nothing. There was absolutely nothing for her to be concerned about. I didn't talk to her for a year and a half and I completely transformed my life. It was clear to me and my twin that her plan was to target me by having others gang up on me and tell me why I'm the problem in family therapy. Once again, she appeared to be this loving, caring, trusting family member that by this time I clearly knew she wasn't, but a new Therapist had no idea. Anything I said in therapy in front of my sister could be fed to my ex-wife and used against me in the custody modification process so opting out was the right move. What was interesting is that after the custody modification process was over, she had no interest in going to family therapy. Narcissists are opportunists any opening they have to get in and break you down they will go after it. The old me would have tried to make an effort in family therapy, but the new me was starting to see the behaviors and tactics. The best way to defend yourself especially in the middle of a smear campaign where you have a lot to lose is to not engage with a narcissistic individual or anyone in frequent contact with that narcissistic individual. This meant no more texts to my sisters' husband either who was a very good friend of mine prior to him meeting and marrying my sister. I told him that I would talk to him and my sister after I was psychologically evaluated again by the Custody Evaluator. I let him know I was already addressing any mental health concerns. I knew it was best to wait for the results from the evaluation to shut down their reality distortions. This proved to be the best strategy.

CHAPTER 11

Malignant Narcissism and Psychopathy

My ex-wife was loving that there was conflict with me and other family members and her dad was ready to pay all of her legal fees for the custody modification process. He had no problem violating people's rights and taking from them. Both of her parents were entitled, nobody was better than them, and they were going to pay her legal fees to get what was theirs. I believe they thought my parenting rights were owned by them. I felt they were in for a rude awakening, but I also knew how hard it was to win against a narcissist in the Court, never mind a series of them, and two of them were my mother and sister. My ex-wife's father is the same guy that fired his sisters' husband and fought him in the

Court on two weeks of unemployment. He told him "I'll do what I have to do to win." His brother-in-law who helped build his business put his place of business down as a reference for potential employers. My ex-wife's father would get on the phone and trash him so he had a very difficult time getting another job when a potential employer would call for a reference. Attempting to put your sister's family on the streets after firing her husband – What type of person would do this? A Malignant Narcissist or Psychopath would. He fired his brother-in-law to make room for his son to come into the business. This was a way to cut the highest salesman's salary, which was $180k and pass it on to his son. He moved his brother-in-law out of the way like he was a chess piece. Ruining a relationship with his sister and brother-in-law didn't matter to him except that it made him look bad, which he couldn't stand because narcissists are always worried about their image and their reputation even though they behave in a manner that ruins it. When my ex-wife's father talked about his brother-in-law not working for him anymore and not having a relationship with his sister he said, "I should have paid him less money." He didn't care that he didn't have a relationship with his sister anymore. It was clear he felt nothing. He was still thinking about how he could have used the guy to make him money. In his eyes he would be useful to him if he just paid him less than the $180k he earned with commission. This is how a narcissist thinks. Narcissists lack object constancy and display conditional love, meaning you are loved for what you do for them not for who you are as a person. You are just an object to be used by them. There should be a warning label when you get into a relationship with a narcissist that reads terms and conditions will apply. Personally, I feel my ex-wife's father crosses over the line to an extremely high number of Psychopath traits, if you were to rate him on the Hare Psychopath Checklist. He would get a check mark for the majority of traits. I've heard it's very hard to distinguish between a malignant narcissist and a psychopath. The two terms are often used interchangeably. It appeared that this is right where my ex-wife and her father were when you break down their personality traits and behavior over time. It's hard to believe that I looked up to him and looked at him as a second father for a period of time.

Speaking of a malignant personality disordered individual, my mother also no longer has a relationship with one of her sisters. In 2002, the two of them started a business where they lost $500,000 in less than six months. They put my grandparent's house up as collateral and if my father didn't pay off the house, they would have lost it. My mother takes no accountability or responsibility for all of debts that had to be paid along with signing for my grandparent's house to be put up as collateral. It wasn't until my 37th birthday in the spring of 2019 I told her if she needed to get a hold of me or leave me a message to call from her house phone or my father's cell phone and that it was no longer appropriate considering the circumstances that we have any cell phone communication. I finally set a firm boundary, she didn't like this. This was one of the best gifts I ever received on a birthday and I gave it to myself. Regardless of how I felt I had to bite my tongue and not tell her how I really felt anymore. If she could feed my ex-wife information that would lead to my time being reduced with my daughter she would. She was already doing this. Everything I thought would happen was happening, that's not paranoia from my understanding. Losing any more time with my daughter than I already had over the past few years wasn't a chance I was willing to take. I knew I had to stay disciplined. Anything I said or did could be used against me. This includes Facebook posts, comments you make to friends or family could all be used against you and twisted to paint you in a negative light in a way you wouldn't believe possible. Narcissists are masters at exploiting you along with executing smear campaigns. They couldn't change how I saw myself, so they continued to try to manipulate how others saw me. The two key people my ex-wife had to attempt to manipulate that I was not a fit father were the Child Psychologist and the Custody Evaluator. These two guys each had over thirty years of experience in dealing with men and women with personality disorders. They also had a great deal of experience as evaluators in high conflict divorces. It was nerve wracking because I heard horror stories of narcissists manipulating the family court system. My ex-wife already successfully manipulated the system once with me. I doubted that these guys had seen a situation where a mother and sister were siding with the high conflict personality disordered parent on the other side. My lawyer said he never saw a situation quite like it.

I was freaking out about how the depositions would impact the custody evaluation. I had a good talk with my lawyer on the phone and he related the situation with the depositions to my days as a Pitcher playing Baseball to calm me down. Both of his brothers played college Baseball where I played.

In reference to the subpoenaing of the text messages, he said, "This is just a scare tactic, step off the mound, take a breath, and focus on the next pitch, it's all about impulse control." He was exactly right. He reminded me that they were not evaluators. At the end of the depositions my lawyer asked them if they had any mental health qualifications. He assured me that their faulty opinions of me meant nothing and he was right.

CHAPTER 12

Psychological Testing and Custody Evaluation

At the end of June 2019, we finally had a Custody Evaluator get involved. My ex-wife met with him first of course so she could attempt to manipulate him. Her strategy was to show the depositions with the text messages from my mom, my sister, and my sisters' husband. I questioned my mom once about the depositions and she mentioned that they put one of my screenshots I texted her, which described what gaslighting was in front of her and asked her if she knew what gaslighting was. I asked her what she said and she told me she didn't know what gaslighting was even though she did it all the time; it was mind boggling. I had multiple conversations with her prior to the depositions explaining to her what gaslighting was. She wasn't capable of comprehending what it was. Her level of insight and awareness was very low.

My ex-wife mentioned to the evaluator that her mother should take care of our daughter over me when I had a great deal of time off in the summer because her mother was more stable than me. There were so many similarities between my ex-wife's mother and my mother. The evaluator told me my ex-wife said, "I'm not sure why Michael would want to have us both evaluated when he has all of these psychological and emotional problems." This is what she told the evaluator. This is exactly what I expected would happen if in fact she was a narcissist that was also psychopathic. When it was my turn to meet with the evaluator, I laid out how the relationship was with my ex-wife during the marriage. He quickly learned I wasn't the person my ex-wife was making me out to be. According to her I was insane, crazy, angry, abusive, dangerous, and not a fit father. I met with him two more times and finally got to show and leave him some documentation of text messages that showed my ex-wife was not willing to let me see my daughter during the day for many weeks over the summer. My documentation showed we did not make decisions together for our daughter's schedule. I also let him know that prior to filing a motion to modify custody I was never notified of medical appointments for our daughter. My ex-wife, her mother, and my mother made a lot of decisions together or the grandmothers would make their own plans through my ex-wife that I was not made aware of at times I was available. This would happen on a regular basis and they would also get together on school vacations when I was free and asking to see our daughter. The current custody plan didn't give me any time during the day in the middle of the week. Being a teacher and having summers off it was difficult to not be able to see my daughter during the day for an entire summer. I let the evaluator know if I didn't go back to Court it was clear this would never change. I had numerous text messages where I would ask if I could spend time with her, she would text back, "Not in our agreement; my mom is going to watch her." This would also happen on snow days when I was off and my daughter was off. At times the roads were passible I let her know I could pick our daughter up but she would reply, "Not in our agreement." These were days my ex-wife still had to work. I left him documentation of all of this. It is imperative that you have proof of these things otherwise it is hearsay and as if it never happened. You know the narcissist will say, "That never happened." With the Custody Evaluator I mainly focused on the positive relationship I had with our daughter and brought in pictures of us together where I could explain the things we enjoyed doing together. He asked me what I thought the custody plan should be. I told him I felt it should be 50/50 physical time unless he could find any reasons it shouldn't be. I let him know I was willing to take on as much time as needed if they found any reasons that it shouldn't be 50/50. You might be asking why I didn't push more time with our daughter. The reason is that even if your ex-spouse is a narcissist, sociopath, or psychopath, they still have rights as parents. If the Custody Evaluator can find no clear reasons to reduce their parenting time, which they probably won't, it will end up 50/50. If I went in there attempting to convince him of all the reasons she was a narcissist, I could have lost time. Instead I focused on the decisions she made that were hurting our daughter and not in her best interest. I also described her narcissistic behaviors without using the term.

During my conversation with the Custody Evaluator, I talked about phrases my ex-wife and my mother would frequently use. They would constantly tell me, "You need help," "You're the problem," "Talk to your Doctor and Therapist," "You're not being honest with your Doctors," "I never said that," "You're imagining things," "You're irrational," "You're paranoid," "You're delusional," "You're Bipolar," "You're insane," and "You're selfish." I also had documentation of them texting me these things. I mentioned to the evaluator I had a therapist that felt my ex-wife was toxic and narcissistic, and I left it at that. I let him know how decisions were made, which was what she said goes. He quickly learned we were dealing with a high conflict personality that was low in agreeableness where it was her way or the highway. I felt he already knew she had a personality disorder but had to meet with her and question her more to know for sure. He needed to meet with her two more times before scheduling the home visits. As part of the evaluation each one of us would have a home visit where the evaluator came out to our home. The visit would last about 2 hours with our daughter.

On 11 August 2019, around the time of the meetings with the evaluator, I stopped at my second cousin's house with our daughter for a play date. His son was going to be in the same class as my daughter for the upcoming school year. I learned from my cousin's wife that my sister contacted them in the fall of 2018 when I had started my new job and things were going well for me. I was taking a low dose of Trazadone and had even talked to them about it since my cousin's wife is a Nurse. My sister texted them and then had a phone conversation that they need to watch out for me because they don't understand how bad things are with me being Bipolar and not taking my medication. My cousin's wife said she felt sick and began to defend me to my sister and gave the phone to my cousin because she was getting very upset. She said that she was uncomfortable about this for a long time and wanted to tell me, but my cousin said not to say anything to prevent conflict in the family, so she didn't. Now that everything was coming to the surface and the truth was coming out with the Custody Evaluator, she felt she should tell me. My cousin and his wife were both references for me in the custody case. I was hurt by the things my sister said to them and wanted to call her out but knew it was best not to. I wasn't surprised by what she did, but it still bothered me quite a bit. Getting stabbed in the back hurts even when you expect it. You get to a certain point where you're sick and tired of getting stabbed in the back even if you are strong enough to take it. I was at the point where none of them could break me. They could stab me in the back as much as they wanted, it didn't affect me as much anymore but it took a long time to get to that point. Knowing what they are capable of I still knew it was best to keep my distance from my sister. It's tough with a covert narcissist like my sister because she did so much damage behind my back it's very difficult to defend against that. Even though I had kept her out of my life for well over a year, she was still finding ways to hurt me and attempt to get people to question my sanity that I wasn't aware of. It's hard to detect it when you don't even know it's happening.

The custody evaluation took a total of 100 days, they are usually 60-90. During the home visit the Custody Evaluator was able to see how comfortable and happy my daughter was with me. She did not appear nervous one bit at my place; she was running around playing Balloon Volleyball with me in our playroom and was so excited when the Evaluator came to the house. She was usually excited when we would get home, but with the Evaluator there she was more excited than usual. The following week I had a therapy appointment with my Therapist.

When I went in for the therapy appointment, he told me he had spoken to the Custody Evaluator earlier that day.

My therapist said, "You're going to come out on top in this thing." He was referring to the custody case.

He also said, "They just need some time to cage this thing." He was referring to my ex-wife when he said this. He was talking about her like she was a great white shark that had been tagged and they were monitoring her behavior except he wasn't referring to a great white shark he was referring to a female psychopath.

The Evaluator also spoke to the first Co-parenting Counselor that we used prior to getting divorced. The Co-parenting Counselor mentioned that she felt my ex-wife had a lot of anger toward me. She also felt that I was not treated properly at the first mental health practice that treated me.

The Evaluator wrote a 40-page report, which was very lengthy according to my lawyer. The Evaluator recommended 50/50 physical custody with the right of first refusal. This would mean that for the days I had off being a teacher my ex-wife would have to give me the first option before pawning her off on other family members. Everything I was looking for was recommended. The report was very thorough and had detailed interviews with any mental health professionals that treated me. The Psychiatric Nurse that was treating me said, "There is no way that Mr. Sunset has Bipolar Disorder." The report showed no form of Bipolar in me that was expected and was a huge relief. Having her evaluated was definitely a difference maker. They got to see who she really was. One of the documents I gave the Evaluator was a screenshot that showed my ex-wife had me in her phone contacts with the name "Zero" on it. The report shows she thinks very little of me as a person and as a parent. That was expected. My sister and my mother were references for my ex-wife. There were notes from phone interviews from them where they were lying and manipulating to get the Evaluator to believe I was Bipolar, unstable, and had periods of going off medication. I let him know this was going to happen, if he talked to them and he saw right through it. There was never a time that I didn't take medication as prescribed. Would I have been better off if I never took any medication in the first place? Possibly, but I'm thankful I found a depression and anxiety medication that was helpful considering the situation. I was anxious, depressed, and had sleep disruptions for a long time. Trazadone is a good medication to treat those symptoms. It was a good temporary solution. I currently do not take any medication after almost 4 years after taking my first dose of a psychotropic medication. There were notes from an in person interview he conducted with my twin brother that gave an honest assessment about our family dynamic. Not everyone has an identical twin to help prove that they are not the person that the manipulators are describing them to be. I love my brother and I'm very thankful to have him. He's been my best friend since we were kids. We'll always be close no doubt about that.

My ex-wife described her childhood as "perfect." Anyone that believes that has a delusional belief in my opinion. A good movie to watch that shows how a narcissistic female that is also psychopathic manipulates the situation to make her spouse out to be somebody he's not is – *Gone Girl.* The only difference with my life is – It wasn't a movie; this seriously just happened to me.

We had an opportunity to settle on the Custody Evaluators recommendations otherwise we would have had to go to a trial that would cost another $20-30k. In the report she said she spent $80k during the divorce process the first time around. I believe this is probably accurate except she wasn't paying for it, her dad was. I would guess that they spent about $110k when it was all said and done. I spent close to $50k altogether, which all went to defending myself from the start. It's very common for a narcissist to run up the bill on legal fees, which means the more they spend the more you will spend. I wonder if they ever look back at the obscene amount of money they blew unneces- sarily and feel foolish at how much of a waste it was. I believe in their minds, they feel it is what they should be doing to "win."

On 28 March 2020, we finally had our settlement meeting, and the three-and-a-half-year battle to get the time my daughter deserved with me would come to an end. The Child Psychologist talked my ex-wife into settling by letting her know there was a 99 percent chance a judge would go off of the Custody Evaluator's recommendations. If she could have fought me on the time she would have. Her goal through this process was to reduce my time and take another shot at getting sole custody, which was evident by her counter motion to reduce my time when I filed my motion to modify.

Her lawyer asked us what we were looking for in terms of custody.

I didn't respond at first and neither did my lawyer. Then I said, "Why don't you guys go first?"

I've learned when you're in a negotiation its best to let the other side show their hand first. The negotiation went well; we ended up settling on just about 50/50 the only change was that my daughter would go back to her on Sunday nights so she would always go to school Monday morning from her place. She agreed to a shared parenting plan with no child support. The right of first refusal was not written in by her lawyer and I was ok with it. My lawyer said they usually stay away from the right of first refusal in high conflict cases prior to our meeting. I was willing to let that go. I couldn't believe it. Our meeting started at 1:00 p.m. and it was over so quickly we were able to walk to the Court house from her lawyer's office and put the agreement in that day. This rarely happens. My lawyer and I figured we would be in for a long day. He said to me, "I thought we would be here all night but this is what happens when you have a plan and do everything right." Part of doing everything right was learning as much as I could about narcissists, sociopaths, and psychopaths. By doing this I was prepared to defend against my ex-wife's behavior along with what to do when my mother and sister would distort reality. One of the most important things were my reactions and responses. By not reacting or responding poorly they will not have much to use against you. It was still stressful and anxiety inducing, but nothing like the divorce process. Her manipulations didn't fool anyone this time. I was also emotionally detached from her this time around that made a big difference. During the divorce process I was giving her emotional reactions because I had a strong emotional attachment to her. When you're emotionally attached it's very hard not to react to a narcissist or other Cluster B when they are abusing you and attempting to provoke an emotional reaction out of you. At this point, the trauma bond with my ex-wife and original trauma bond with my mother has been completely shattered, and it's a great feeling when you get to that point.

CHAPTER 13

Healing and Recovering

A huge part of the recovery and healing process for me was to educate myself as much as I could about narcissists, sociopaths, psychopaths, and borderlines. If I hadn't done this, I wouldn't be where I am today. I wouldn't wish my experience on anyone, but there are so many people out there that have had similar experiences that are looking for answers in regard to what happened to them and what to do next. I currently still see the same Therapist that was trying to tell me I was being abused back in March 2016. He helped me to rebuild trust with myself along with be compassionate towards myself. I blamed myself for everything and he also helped me to forgive myself. He introduced me to mindfulness meditation and taught me diaphragmatic breathing. It didn't do much for me in the beginning but the more I did it the more focused and grounded in the present moment I became. The more I meditated the quicker my thoughts would turn from the past or distracted back to the present. This really helped me go from feeling disconnected to becoming more grounded and connected. I could feel this shift taking place. Now that I have put the worst of this situation behind me, I can feel real healing starting to take place. On 4 March 2020, my daughter fell asleep in her room without me staying in there sitting in a chair after reading to her for the first time since she was unfairly ripped away from me in August of 2016. She said, "It's ok dad you can shut the light off and close the door." This allowed me to start sleeping more peacefully.

I listened to guided sleep meditations for about 4 years straight almost every night to fall asleep. These were guided meditations for sleep, anxiety, depression, overthinking, ruminating thoughts, letting go, self-love, and healing. I still listen to them many nights. After all of the gaslighting and negative messages my mind took in, this allows for positive messages to fill my head while I sleep. It's very helpful. Everyone's treatment and recovery will be different. Nobody has been through the exact same abuse, but if you have been a victim of narcissistic abuse it does leave a similar imprint that I feel each person that has been through it can relate to. One of the biggest issues is being in the middle of it and not knowing exactly what you're dealing with. It's important to get out, educate yourself about it, and observe it for what it is. That is enough to not want to go back. If you're still in frequent contact with your abuser, you are preventing yourself from beginning the healing process. You'll find the more time away from that abuser or abusers the calmer and more stable you will become. It's important to distance yourself and limit your contact, if you can't make a clean break. If you can make a clean break, you should do it so you don't go through any more pain and suffering than you already have. It may be helpful to write a goodbye letter and say everything you would want to say to that person in the letter but do not give it to them. Focus on self-care and what you need to do each day and night to be healthy.

When healing from one of these relationships I think it's important to have at least one trusted friend or family member you can count on and talk to regularly. Not the narcissistic ones that are pretending to help you like my situation. I would also suggest getting involved in hobbies that you used to enjoy whether its writing, drawing, painting, walking, hiking, swimming, walking the dog, traveling, working out, or doing yoga to name a few. If you already have activities in place keep participating in them. Whatever pieces of you that were taken away get those pieces back and start doing something you never did before on top of it. It's important to be active if possible and exercise. Breaking a sweat a few times a week will help with the psychological and emotional struggles you are going through or went through. I'm hoping for a healthy recovery for anyone dealing with or recovering from this type of abuse. I'm aware I still have healing work that needs to be done and I'm not done yet. If I'm able to help one person to free themselves from this type of abuse by writing this book, then it was worth it to me! It's hard to believe that a group of people I loved from my wife's family and my own family could psychologically and emotionally abuse me to the point that I became suicidal, but I know I'm not the first person this has happened to and I'm not going to be the last. I'm living proof that you can overcome it. I believe I was targeted because I had money, friends, a strong sense of integrity, a great sense of humor, am honest, trustworthy, reliable, intuitive, caring, loyal, empathetic, compassionate, and a well-rounded person. A narcissist will erode your self-esteem and wear you down where you and others won't recognize the amazing person you used to be. It's important to remember you are still that person and you can create an even better version of yourself. None of us have to be victims anymore. We can all be survivors, start thriving, and become stronger as a result. I never knew what an empath was but it appears I fit the description really well. I also learned that I have an INFJ personality type which is very rare for males. Being an empath and having an INFJ personality makes a person a prime target for a narcissist. With my teaching position teaching at a special needs school I've been able to surround myself with many highly empathetic people. It's a much more supportive environment compared to where I grew up and my marriage. It is important to connect with truly supportive and caring people.

As I am finishing this book, it is Easter Sunday 2020, our country is shut down due the corona virus COVID-19. Just like narcissistic individuals we have to learn to live with and be aware of the dangers of this virus being all around us. We are being told that the way to beat the virus is through "social distancing." I feel this also applies to the narcissistic individuals in society as well. The more we can distance ourselves, limit our contact, and reduce exposure to them the greater our overall health will be. The time being shut down has allowed me to spend quality time with my daughter and assist her with her school assignments after losing so much time with her.

I believe that a narcissist's behavior doesn't have anything to do with the person they are hurting it is a reflection of who they are. They are hurting and, as a result, will hurt the people closest to them. Knowing this it is much easier to take the steps to break free and move on with your life without that narcissistic individual in it. Their behavior won't change so it's important for the victims, targets, and survivors to make changes. It can definitely be done. Remember to focus on the positives in your life, build on them, and to keep moving forward!